101 Things You Need to Know About...

The Titanic

by
Tim O'Shei

kidsbooks

Photo Credits

AP/Wide World: cover/p. 3; pp. 34, 35, 36-37, 38-39, 40-41, 42-43

The Father Browne Photographic Collection: pp. 6-7, 11, 12, 13, 17, 18, 19, 20, 21, 24

Getty Images, Inc.: p. 30

The Granger Collection: pp. 4, 14, 15, 16, 25, 26, 28-29, 31

The Kobal Collection: p. 41

The Library of Congress Prints and Photographs Division: pp. 8, 22-23, 26, 27, 32 (both), 33, 46-47, 48

The Ulster Folk and Transport Museum: pp. 9, 10, 14

Visit us at **www.kidsbooks.com**

Welcome to the Titanic

Are you ready to take a ride through history?

Are you ready to step aboard a floating palace, a ship full of dazzling riches and spooky secrets?

Are you ready to face the icy-cold facts—all 101 of them?

If you are ready to learn, then welcome aboard. We are taking a trip back to 1912 as well as a voyage to the bottom of the ocean. We are going to visit one of the greatest ships ever built, and relive one of the most famous tragedies in history.

We are going to the *Titanic*.

Enjoy your time aboard this ship, which once was the finest—and became the most famous—ever built.

Just have a life jacket handy, and keep an eye on the lifeboats. You are going to need them!

Questions You Would Probably Ask Anyway
(so we'll answer them first)

How many people were aboard the *Titanic?*

1. Some historians say 2,224. Others insist on more. The truth is, we will never really know. No passenger list is known to be completely accurate.

How long was the *Titanic* supposed to take to reach New York?

2. Seven days. It left Southampton, England, on Wednesday, April 10, 1912, and was expected to arrive in New York on Wednesday, April 17.

How long did the White Star Line's managing director want the trip to take?

3. Six days. J. Bruce Ismay wanted the *Titanic* to arrive in New York earlier than expected. That way, the grand ship's arrival would make newspaper headlines, and he would be famous. Many people think that Ismay ordered the captain to speed up the ship for that reason.

When did the *Titanic's* watch officers spot the iceberg?

4. At approximately 11:40 p.m. on April 14, 1912.

How fast was the *Titanic* traveling when the iceberg was spotted?

5. Twenty-two knots (about 25 miles per hour). For a ship of that time, that was full speed.

How long did the officer commanding the bridge that evening have to react to the iceberg warning?

6. Not much. First Officer William Murdoch had just 37 seconds.

What did Murdoch do?

7. To slow the ship, he ordered the *Titanic*'s propellers to be put in reverse. He also had the ship turn sharply to the left. There still wasn't enough time to avoid the collision.

When was the last lifeboat lowered into the water?

8. At 2:05 a.m. on April 15, 1912.

When did the *Titanic* sink?

9. The last part of the ship sank at 2:20 a.m. on April 15, 1912.

How many lifeboats did the *Titanic* have?

10. It had 16 wooden lifeboats plus four collapsibles (wooden rafts with canvas sides). Collapsibles took up less deck space than regular lifeboats, because they could be stored flat. When needed, they could be unfolded and locked into place.

How many people were those lifeboats meant to hold?

11. Only 1,178—about half of the people on the ship.

How many people did those lifeboats actually hold?

12. All told, the *Titanic*'s lifeboats carried only 705 survivors—fewer than one third of the ship's passenger load.

How many people died?

13. The number that most historians agree on is 1,522.

Where did all this happen?

14. The location of the shipwreck is 41° North latitude, 49° West longitude. That is about 400 miles off the coast of the Canadian province of Newfoundland.

stern

Terms You Will Be Glad to Know as You Read This Book

15. The main body or frame of a ship—its sides, bottom, and decks—is called the **hull.** (The *hull* does not include smokestacks, engines, and other parts of a ship.)

16. The front end of a ship is called the **bow, prow** (both rhyme with *how*), or **stem.** The rear end is called the **stern.**

17. When you are on a ship and facing forward (toward the ship's bow), the right-hand side is called **starboard** and the left-hand side is called **port.**

18. The **bridge** is the area of a ship where the captain works. It is where commands are given, decisions on the ship's speed and direction are made, and warnings are delivered.

19. Set toward the ship's bow is a very tall pole with a two-person perch about a third of the way up. In that perch, called the **crow's nest,** officers stand duty 24 hours a day, searching the horizon for possible dangers—such as icebergs.

smokestack

bridge

crow's nest

bow

hull

Meet the White Star Sisters
(How it all began)

sister ships: the *Olympic* is at left, the *Titanic* at right

Floating family

20. In 1907, the White Star Line set plans to build three luxury ships. Construction on the first two, the *Olympic* and the *Titanic*, began the following year. A third ship, the *Brittanic*, was built later.

The big sister

21. The *Olympic* came first. It was launched on October 20, 1910. It wasn't quite as big as the *Titanic*, but it lasted much longer. (It operated until 1935.) When the *Olympic* was dismantled, many of its decorations were sold. At the White Swan Hotel in Alnwick, England, you can see wooden paneling from the ship. Historians and filmmakers have gone there to learn more about the interior design of *Titanic*, because the sister ships were so similar.

the *Titanic* under construction

Don't believe everything you see

22. Very little film of the *Titanic* exists. Many times, when a documentary shows the *Titanic*, what you actually are seeing is the *Olympic*.

The little sister

23. The *Britannic* had a short life, too. On November 12, 1916, a couple of years after its launch, it sank in the Aegean Sea, near a Greek island. This happened during World War I. The cause, most historians agree, was an underwater mine or a torpedo. The passengers were luckier than the *Titanic*'s: Only 30 of 1,000 of them died.

Feel Free to Show Off!

A dressed-up society

24. The *Titanic* sailed during what is known as "The Gilded Age." It was a time when wealthy people would dress up in expensive clothes and jewelry, and take long, exotic vacations. Although they were to be on the ship for only seven days, most of the *Titanic*'s first-class passengers took several trunks of clothing and belongings.

A big-time project

25. More than 15,000 workers spent two years building the *Titanic* at the Harlan & Wolff shipyard in Belfast, Ireland. When finished, the ship weighed 66,000 tons and was 882.5 feet long—the length of almost three football fields. The *Titanic* was powered by four steam engines, each of which was the size of a three-story house.

first-class elevators on the *Titanic*

February 1912, Belfast, Ireland: the *Titanic* in dry dock, under construction and nearly complete

World record

26. At the time of its launch, the *Titanic* was the largest human-made moving object ever built.

Now that is horsepower!

27. It took 20 horses to haul the *Titanic*'s anchor through the streets of Belfast to the ship.

Don't blow this stack

28. The *Titanic* had four smokestacks (also called funnels). Only three worked, discharging smoke and gases. The fourth was just for decoration.

 Bon Voyage!

A short test

29. The *Titanic*'s test voyage lasted less than a day. On the morning of April 2, 1912, the ship's equipment was tested for starting, stopping, and turning. The wireless radio—the same one that would send out distress calls 12 days later—was tested, too. That first voyage was a short one: The *Titanic* sped 40 miles out into the Irish Sea, then turned around and went straight back to the dock at Belfast, Ireland. At 8 p.m., just 14 hours after the testing began, the *Titanic* left Belfast and sailed 570 miles to Southampton, England, where the first passengers boarded the ship.

Father Browne's photo of passengers boarding the ship at Southampton

Father Browne's photo of a crowd on the wharf at Queenstown, awaiting the *Titanic*'s arrival

A few quick stops

30. The *Titanic* began its maiden (first) voyage at noon on Wednesday, April 10, 1912, when it left Southampton, England. At 6:30 that evening, it arrived at Cherbourg, France, where more passengers boarded. The next day, after a final stop at Queenstown, Ireland, the *Titanic* entered the open ocean and headed for New York. It never saw land again.

Final photos

31. Few photographs taken aboard the *Titanic* exist. Those that do were the work of Father Francis Browne, a priest who boarded the ship at Southampton. He traveled only to Cherbourg and back to Ireland, going ashore at Queenstown. Without realizing it, he had captured moments in history that otherwise would have been lost forever.

the *Titanic*'s Café Parisienne, for first-class passengers

HI733.
R.W.

Separating the classes

32. First-, second-, and third-class passengers were kept separate from each other. Each class had its own sections of the ship in which to eat, sleep, and have fun. First class had the most luxurious surroundings. But even third-class areas (also known as steerage) on the *Titanic* were clean and comfortable, compared with those of other ships of the day.

The richest passenger

33. John Jacob Astor was the wealthiest man aboard. (His great-grandfather, who had the same name, had been the richest man in the U.S.) Astor and his wife, Madeleine, had spent the winter in Egypt and France, and were heading home to New York. Traveling with them were Mr. Astor's servant, Mrs. Astor's maid, a nurse, and their dog, Kitty. The women survived. The men and dog did not.

The captain's good-bye

34. The *Titanic*'s captain, Edward J. Smith, was one of the most famous and respected sea captains in the world. He planned to retire after the *Titanic*'s grand maiden voyage. What Smith expected to be the final voyage of his long and honored career turned out to be the final voyage of his life.

the *Titanic*, about to leave Southampton (note that no smoke is coming from the rear, fake smokestack)

🚢 Welcome 🚢 to the Palace

The White Star's big star

35. White Star Line advertised the *Titanic* as a "floating palace."

A top-dollar trip

36. A first-class ticket on the *Titanic* cost $4,300. In today's money, that is about $50,000!

Taking grand steps

37. One of the most famous spots on the *Titanic* was the Grand Staircase. It featured elaborate wooden paneling, a fancy clock, and a glass ceiling. The clock played a bit part in the 1997 movie *Titanic*. Third-class passenger Jack Dawson (played by Leonardo DiCaprio) slips a note to the first-class girl he has a crush on, Rose DeWitt Bukater (Kate Winslet). The message: "Make it count. Meet me at the clock." She does, and they fall in love. The rest is movie history.

the *Olympic*'s Grand Staircase, which was a twin of the *Titanic*'s

Water on deck!

38. The *Titanic* and its sister ship, the *Olympic*, had swimming pools on board. This may not seem like such a big deal today, but it was a rare luxury back in 1912.

The ultimate workout

39. First-class passengers had two main ways to get some exercise aboard the *Titanic.* The first was getting dressed: Many of them changed their clothes up to six times per day! (This was the Gilded Age, remember. People liked to show off their impressive outfits.) The other was working out in the on-board gym, which had equipment that was cutting-edge—for 1912. Among the workout devices aboard were punching bags, rowing machines, exercise bikes, and a mechanical horse.

Lots of food

40. Each member of the kitchen staff had his or her own specialty, from soups to meats to pastries. They prepared 4,000 meals a day! That required a huge stockpile of food, which included 40,000 eggs and 36,000 apples.

the *Titanic*'s state-of-the-art gymnasium

Hungry?

41. The *Titanic*'s first-class passengers enjoyed the same fancy foods that they could get in any expensive restaurant ashore: lobster, quail, caviar (fish eggs), and other top-dollar foodstuffs.

42. Offerings on the second-class menu included spaghetti, corned beef, sausage, tapioca pudding, and ox tongue.

43. Third-class passengers were given a breakfast that included oatmeal, bacon, liver, rabbit, and bread.

below: **the first-class dining room;** *right:* **the meal served there a few hours before the ship hit an iceberg**

R.M.S. *TITANIC*

April 14, 1912
FIRST-CLASS SERVICE
DINNER

Shrimp canapés and raw oysters with vodka, lemon, and hot sauce

Consommé or barley soup

Poached salmon with mousseline sauce

A CHOICE OF
Filet mignon with foie gras and black truffles
or chicken Lyonnaise
OR
Minted lamb, glazed roast duck or beef sirloin,
served with potatoes, mint tea timbales,
and creamed carrots

Sorbet made from champagne, orange juice, and rum

Roast squab on watercress

Asparagus-champagne-saffron salad

Chocolate éclairs, French vanilla ice cream or jellied
peaches, assorted fresh fruits and cheeses

19

Father Browne's photo of the children's playground

Just relax!

44. After dinner, the men in first class would gather in the smoking room, chatting over cigars and glasses of brandy. The women stayed in the dining area, chatting over cups of tea, or returned to their rooms to relax. Other leisure hours were often spent outdoors, with children playing on deck while adults took strolls or stretched out in deck chairs.

Animals aboard!

45. Passengers who took pets aboard the *Titanic* left them in the ship's kennel. When the ship began to sink, one of the passengers went to the kennel and opened the cages. Two dogs made it into lifeboats and survived.

Spooky, but True

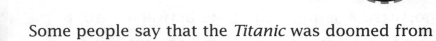

That tiny dot at the top of the ship's last smokestack was a worker. But superstitious people who didn't know that the smokestack was a fake thought they were seeing an evil spirit.

Some people say that the *Titanic* was doomed from the start. Were these coincidences—or warnings?

46. In a novel called *The Wreck of the Titan*, an "unsinkable" ship, the *Titan*, leaves England for the U.S. Many rich and famous people are aboard. The ship strikes an iceberg and sinks, and many people die because there are not enough lifeboats. The weird thing is, author Morgan Robertson published his book in 1898—14 years before the *Titanic* set sail!

47. While workers were loading coal into the *Titanic* at Southampton, a fire started. Men fought it around the clock, but it was not put out—until the ship sank.

48. Henry Wilde, chief officer aboard the *Titanic*, sent a message to his sister, saying, "I still don't like this ship. I have [an odd] feeling about it."

49. As the *Titanic* left Southampton, it traveled down a narrow channel. A nearby ship, the *New York*, got pulled into the channel by water churned up by the *Titanic*'s powerful propellers. Tugboats pulled the *New York* back before the two ships could collide. That was the *Titanic*'s last lucky break.

⚓ "Iceberg ⚓ Right Ahead!"

How could a ship as big as the *Titanic* hit an object as big as an iceberg? These are some of the problems that led up to the fateful crash.

50. The winter of 1911-1912 had been unusually warm, causing icebergs along the coast of Greenland to break apart and drift south. By April, ice fields were scattered across the northern Atlantic—the route between Europe and North America traveled by many ships, including the *Titanic*.

51. Throughout the day and night leading up to the collision, the *Titanic*'s crew received seven ice warnings from other ships traveling in the Atlantic. One of the officers examined the warnings and concluded that the ice fields were safely north of the *Titanic*'s route. He was wrong.

52. The last warning was never delivered to Captain Smith. Sent from a ship called the *Californian*, it said, "I say, old man, we're stopped and surrounded by ice." It came in while Jack Phillips, a radio operator, was sending messages from *Titanic* passengers to friends back home. His annoyed reply to the *Californian* was, "I'm busy!"

53. On the night of April 14, 1912, the air was calm and cold, and the Atlantic was smooth as glass. There was no wind to splash waves against icebergs, and no moonlight to make such waves visible.

54. At 11:40 p.m., Watch Officer Fred Fleet saw a huge iceberg directly in the *Titanic*'s path. From the crow's nest, he called the bridge and screamed, "Iceberg right ahead!"

55. Immediately, the *Titanic*'s officers reversed the engines and tried to turn the ship away from the iceberg. It was too late. The ship's side scraped along the iceberg, punching holes in the hull and spilling water inside.

an iceberg at sea

🚂 Disaster! 🚂

The moment the ship scraped the iceberg, things on board seemed to go from bad to worse.

56. When the *Titanic* struck, chunks of ice fell onto the third-class promenade deck. A few boys, not realizing the danger they were in, began kicking the ice around, as a game. Soon, though, some third-class families came onto the deck, carrying all their belongings. They knew what the ice meant: trouble.

57. In Morse code, a universally understood signaling system, each letter has its own pattern of short clicks (dots) and long clicks (dashes). The emergency signal SOS is spelled • • • — — — • • •. In 1912, SOS (short for "save our souls") was a new term. The *Titanic*'s radio operators were among the first to use it.

58. The *Californian* was only about 10 miles away, but its radio officer had turned off his equipment and headed to bed at 11:35 p.m.—just five minutes before the *Titanic*'s crash. That left no one to hear the pleas for help.

59. One of the first parts of the ship to flood was the mail room. Instead of trying to escape, the five postal workers stationed there tried to save the letters by moving them to a higher, drier deck. They failed to save the mail—or themselves.

Father Browne's photo of the *Titanic*'s radio room

60. Shipbuilder Thomas Andrews designed the *Titanic*'s hull with water-tight compartments. If the first four filled with water, the ship could stay afloat. In this case, though, water was streaming into five. Scientists have been analyzing the accident ever since. Many of them believe that if the *Titanic* had hit the iceberg head-on, only the front compartments would have been damaged and the ship would have stayed afloat. With a sideswipe, however, the damage was spread too far and wide.

**one artist's idea of
the fateful collision**

To the Lifeboats!

In the dark

61. After the *Titanic* struck the iceberg and its engines halted, rumors started to spread around the ship. One was that the *Titanic* had stopped to avoid hitting an iceberg. Another was that the ship had lost a propeller blade. At first, only Captain Edward Smith, J. Bruce Ismay (head of the White Star Line), Thomas Andrews (the *Titanic*'s designer), and a few other people realized how badly the ship had been damaged.

Into the lifeboats!

62. The first passengers to board the *Titanic*'s lifeboats were the women and children. Credit for that gentlemanly plan goes to Officer Charles Lightoller. He suggested it to Captain Smith, who agreed. "Women and children first" became an international rule of rescue.

Titanic lifeboats arriving at the Carpathia

True love

63. When Ida Straus was offered a place on a lifeboat, she turned it down. She chose to stay with her husband, Isador Straus, so they could die together. (Isador Straus was co-owner of Macy's, a world-famous New York department store.)

Unladylike behavior

64. The women-and-children-first rule did not stop some men from climbing into lifeboats. Rumor has it that one passenger, Daniel Buckley, covered his head with a shawl to look like a woman.

the sinking of the *Titanic*,
recreated for a Hollywood movie

The Ship Is Sinking!

Out of touch

65. Even as they were boarding lifeboats, many first- and second-class passengers didn't realize how bad things were. They hadn't seen the flooding in the lower decks. Many of them thought that they would go back aboard as soon as a problem was fixed. One man told his daughter that he would see her for breakfast in the morning, not realizing that they would never see each other again.

Gentlemen to the end

66. Among the ship's passengers was Benjamin Guggenheim, a millionaire, and his valet. When the two men realized that there was not room in the lifeboats for everyone aboard, they dressed in fancy tuxedos and went to the first-class smoking room. "We are dressed up in our best," Guggenheim said, "and prepared to go down like gentlemen." Both men went down with the ship.

Background music

67. At the captain's request, the *Titanic*'s band began playing upbeat ragtime music soon after the troubles started. The band kept playing until shortly before the ship went down, and all of its members died. They are considered heroes for trying to calm frightened passengers trapped in a deadly situation. The last song that the band played was a hymn, "Nearer, My God, to Thee."

Light hope

68. Some *Titanic* officers saw a white light in the distance. It seemed to be a steamship about five miles away. Unable to contact the mystery ship by radio, at 12:45 a.m. they began to shoot rockets into the air. Although that distress signal failed to lure the other ship to their rescue, it did convince the *Titanic*'s passengers that the ship was going down.

Empty seats

69. Although the *Titanic*'s 1,178 lifeboat seats were enough for only half the people on the ship, there were more lifeboats than the number required by law. Even so, 472 of those lifeboats seats were never used.

Should the boss have stayed?

70. J. Bruce Ismay, head of the White Star Line, wanted the *Titanic* to make headlines. He got his headlines, but not the way he had wanted. Many people blamed Ismay for more than the disaster itself. They also criticized him for a choice that he made while the ship was sinking. After helping many people onto lifeboats, Ismay climbed into the final boat on his side of the ship. No one else was around, so Ismay was not taking another passenger's spot. Later, however, people said that since he was responsible for the ship, he should have stayed aboard and gone down with it.

a 1912 illustration drawn for a London newspaper

Going down

71. As the bow of the *Titanic* filled with water, it dipped lower and lower into the ocean, and the stern tipped upward. Eventually, the weight of the stern above became so heavy that the ship broke apart between the third and fourth smokestacks. While the bow sank to the ocean floor, the stern bobbed at the surface for a while as water flooded into it. Within a few minutes, the stern sank, too.

Uneven survival

72. *Titanic* legend has it that third-class passengers were locked behind gates while upper-class passengers boarded lifeboats that were lowered before they were filled. Did it really happen? Historians don't know, but they agree that many more steerage passengers died than first- or second-class passengers. Seventy-five percent of the *Titanic*'s third-class passengers lost their lives, while fewer than 50 percent of the first- and second-class ticket holders died.

The lucky one

73. The only person to be recovered by a lifeboat from the icy water after the *Titanic* went down was Charles Joughin, a baker on the ship.

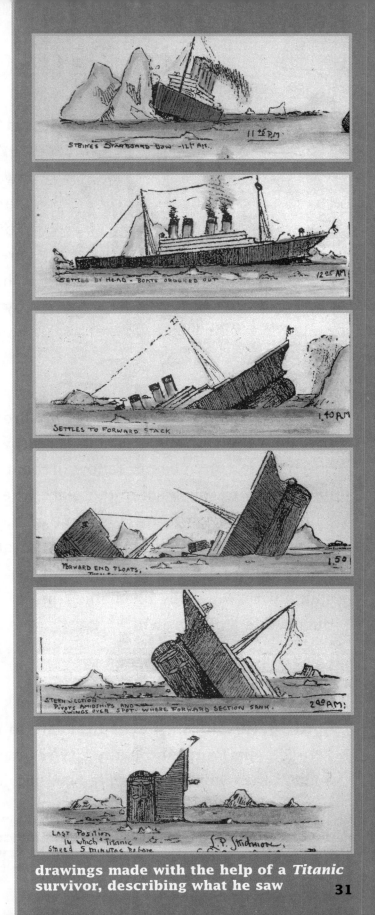

drawings made with the help of a *Titanic* survivor, describing what he saw

Rescue!

Help at last

74. At 4 a.m. on April 15, a little under two hours after the *Titanic* sank, a ship named the *Carpathia* arrived at the scene. For most of the morning, the *Carpathia*'s crew lifted the lifeboats onto their ship. The 705 *Titanic* survivors were welcomed by *Carpathia*'s passengers, who shared their cabins, blankets, and dry clothing.

the *Carpathia*

No keeping her down

75. One *Titanic* survivor was Molly Brown, the rich widow of businessman J. J. Brown. She tried to convince her fellow lifeboat passengers to row back to the place where the ship had gone down, to save some of the people who were drowning in the icy water. She could not get them to do it, but her spunk earned her the nickname "the Unsinkable Molly Brown."

New York, New York

76. The *Carpathia* arrived in New York on April 18. Hospitals gave medical care to the *Titanic*'s survivors, and many city residents opened their homes to people who had lost everything.

the "Unsinkable" Molly Brown, leaving the *Carpathia* in New York after the rescue

🚂 The 🚂 Aftermath

Recovery efforts

77. During the six weeks that followed the sinking of the *Titanic*, many ships went to the disaster site to search for bodies. Only 328 were recovered.

Covering the burial

78. Many of the bodies that were recovered are buried in a cemetery in England. The cost of the burial and upkeep of the graves was covered by the White Star Line.

Changing the rules

79. Investigations by the governments of both Britain and the U.S. resulted in stricter passenger-safety rules for ships. More lifeboats were required, and dangerous icy areas were to be more carefully patrolled.

lucky ones: a family who survived the sinking of the *Titanic*

A Return to the *Titanic*

Wanted: the *Titanic*

80. For more than seven decades, scientists, explorers, and treasure hunters longed to find the sunken *Titanic*. Dr. Robert D. Ballard, an American scientist who loves underwater exploration, had had that dream since the mid-1970s. It took him nearly 10 years to convince others to join him, but his dream project finally got under-way. In the summer of 1985, Ballard set out with Jean-Louis Michel, a French explorer, to find the fallen ship.

An *Argo*'s-eye view

81. In a research ship named the *Knorr*, Ballard, Michel, and their crew traveled to the area where the *Titanic* went down. Then they scoured the floor of the northern Atlantic using *Argo*, a steel sled fitted with video cameras—and a cable 2.5 miles long. As they dragged *Argo* along, Ballard and Michel watched their video screens, looking for signs of a shipwreck.

Robert Ballard with *Jason Junior*

the bow of the wrecked *Titanic*

Boiling up a clue

82. With only four days of their six-week expedition left, Ballard and Michel had found nothing. Then, on September 1, 1985, a discovery: The crew spotted a stream of man-made items, including a boiler plate. They checked what they had seen against a book of *Titanic* pictures. They matched perfectly!

The *Titanic* found!

83. By following the path of debris, Ballard, Michel, and their crew soon reached the hull of the *Titanic*. The long-lost ship had been found at last—73 years after it went down.

Thrills, then sorrow

84. **Finding the *Titanic* fulfilled a lifelong goal for Ballard. But he and the crew realized that they had found a grave site as well as a ship. More than 1,500 people had died there. The explorers gathered on the deck of the *Knorr* for a short memorial service. For months after the discovery, Ballard was so affected by thoughts of the 1912 tragedy that he would not talk about the *Titanic*.**

Worldwide headlines

85. **Suddenly, the *Titanic* was back in the news. The wreck's discovery got worldwide attention. On September 9, when the *Knorr* docked at Nantucket Sound, Massachusetts, it was mobbed by reporters and tourists.**

the *Alvin (below, at left)* exploring the *Titanic's* hull

Going back for more

86. In July 1986, Ballard returned to the northern Atlantic. (Michel could not join the second expedition.) Ballard's plan was to examine the ship up close. To do that, he would travel to the ocean floor in a submersible—a craft designed for deep-sea research.

A long way down

87. It took two and a half hours for the *Alvin*, Ballard's submersible, to reach the ocean floor. The trip was made in near darkness, because Ballard and his crew didn't use any power inside the *Alvin* on the way down. They wanted to save it for exploring as long as possible, and for rising back to the surface.

Alvin on the blink

88. On Ballard's first deep-sea visit to the *Titanic*, the *Alvin*'s battery was leaking. Ballard got only a glimpse of the ship's hull before having to return to the surface.

No swimming here!

89. For Robert Ballard and everyone else who has visited the *Titanic* after him, safety has been a top concern. At 13,000 feet under the sea, the water pressure is so great that the smallest crack in a submersible's wall can cause the entire vessel to burst inward. That would kill everyone inside instantly.

A longer look

90. On July 14, 1986—in a repaired *Alvin*—Ballard returned to the *Titanic*. That time, he and his two crew members were able to explore the ship in detail. They landed in a couple of spots and hovered over others. To capture images, they used a remote-controlled underwater robot, called *Jason Junior*. (You have already met *Jason Junior*. Take another look at the object that appears with Ballard in the photo on page 34.)

Uncommon icicles

91. The wreck of the *Titanic* is covered with streams of brownish-red rust. Ballard came up with a new word for those icicle-shaped formations: *rusticles*.

Split proof

92. As the *Titanic* was sinking, did it break into two pieces? That question had been a matter of debate for decades. Photos taken by Robert Ballard finally settled the question: It had. The bow and stern were about 2,000 feet apart on the ocean floor.

Honoring the dead

93. Ballard wanted to leave a tribute to the people who died on the *Titanic*. He had a plaque strapped to the outside of the *Alvin*, carrying it to the sea bottom. He then used the craft's mechanical arm to leave it on the stern of the *Titanic*.

"rusticles" crusting
the *Titanic*'s bow

Leave It or Take It?

A grim reminder

94. **A shipwreck is a great temptation. Robert Ballard once thought of taking artifacts from his great find—until he saw a pair of shoes. For Ballard, that simple human touch was a powerful reminder that the *Titanic* is more than just a rusting hunk of metal. "I just felt it's not my right to disturb this site," Ballard has said. He has refused to take anything from the wreck ever since.**

Museum works

95. **Not everyone feels the way Ballard does about the *Titanic* wreckage. Since Ballard's 1985 discovery, more than 4,000 artifacts have been recovered from the wreck site, including dishes, clocks, jewelry, statues, and a piece of a door. Most of the items are on display in museums around the world.**

Up for grabs

96. **When explorers find a shipwreck, they usually claim exclusive rights to it. If the claim is granted, no one else will be allowed to remove objects from the wreck without permission from the finder. When Ballard found the *Titanic*, however, he did not stake a claim, so he has no say in what happens to it. He now regrets not claiming ownership. "I didn't think all this would happen," he has said of explorers taking things from the site.**

Treasure hunting

97. **George Tulloch, an underwater explorer, was one of the people who have taken objects from the wreck. Tulloch headed a company called RMS Titanic Inc., which has collected *Titanic***

This photo, taken in July 2003, shows what is left of the captain's cabin: water pipes and the bathtub.

an employee of George Tulloch's company prepares a section of the *Titanic*'s raised hull for an exhibit

You have to spend money to make money

98. A trip to the ocean floor is hugely expensive. Tulloch's plunges to the ocean floor inside his submersible, the *Nautile*, cost about $5 per second—$100,000 per dive. To help cover the cost of exploring the *Titanic*, Tulloch's company helped pay that steep price by selling coal from the ship. In on-line auctions, the starting price for coal from the *Titanic* is around $15 a piece.

Rise and shine!

99. In Tulloch's explorations of the shipwreck, he found a 23-foot, 20-ton section of the *Titanic*'s hull. Knowing that it would be an irresistible museum draw, he was determined to bring it to the surface. His plan was to attach giant lift bags, filled with diesel fuel, to the hull piece, then float it to the surface. When he and his crew tried it in 1996, it worked. That success, though, raised another problem: Once Tulloch and the crew got the hull piece to the surface, they weren't able to secure it with cable. In 1998, they tried again. That time, they managed to float the hull piece and harness it by cable. For the first time in 86 years, the *Titanic*—a piece of it, anyway—was seeing the light of day.

A Story That Will Live Forever

Rebuilding the *Titanic* 100. To film his 1997 blockbuster film *Titanic*, director James Cameron had the interior of the ship recreated in precise detail. His staff consulted the ship designer's original blueprints to make sure that their *Titanic* was a perfect match. The movie ship's exterior was another model, built at 90 percent of the real ship's size. A hydraulic system was used to tilt it up and down, as if on waves. This model was housed in a 17-million-gallon water tank. Another water tank, holding 5 million gallons, was used to film the flood scenes of *Titanic*'s interior.

The Last Word

101. **The story of the *Titanic*'s first and only voyage has fascinated
every generation since the day the ship went down. The *Titanic* has been
the subject of countless articles, as well as many books, TV programs,
and movies. Although the great ship is no more, its story will never die.**

Titanic Quiz:
How shipshape are you?

1. **Who was the captain of the *Titanic*?**
   a. John Jacob Astor
   b. Jack Dawson
   c. J. Bruce Ismay
   d. Edward Smith

2. **What was the name of the *Titanic*'s older sister ship?**
   a. the *Britannic*
   b. the *Californian*
   c. the *Carpathia*
   d. the *Olympic*

3. **What was the name for the time period during which people showed off their wealth?**
   a. the Gilded Age
   b. the Golden Era
   c. the Reign of the Rich
   d. the Show-off Society

4. **Where was the *Titanic* supposed to dock at the end of its maiden voyage?**
   a. Cherbourg, France
   b. New York, U.S.A.
   c. Queenstown, Ireland
   d. Southampton, England

5. **What is the name of the ship in Morgan Robertson's novel that is eerily similar to the actual story of the *Titanic*?**
   a. the *Titan*
   b. the *Titania*
   c. the *Titannica*
   d. the *Tremendous*

6. **How much time did First Officer William Murdoch have to react between learning of the iceberg ahead and colliding with it?**
   a. 22 seconds
   b. 37 seconds
   c. 45 seconds
   d. 66 seconds

7. **Which ship was close to the sinking of the *Titanic* but never heard its distress calls?**
   a. the *Californian*
   b. the *Carpathia*
   c. the *Lusitania*
   d. the *New York*

8. **Who designed and oversaw the construction of the _Titanic_?**
   a. Thomas Andrews
   b. Benjamin Guggenheim
   c. J. Bruce Ismay
   d. Edward Smith

9. **Who was the wealthy _Titanic_ passenger who became famous and known by the nickname "Unsinkable"?**
   a. Madeleine Astor
   b. Molly Brown
   c. Rose DeWitt Bukater
   d. Ida Straus

10. **What was the name of the submersible vessel used by Robert Ballard when he went underwater to visit the _Titanic_ in 1986?**
    a. the _Alvin_
    b. _Jason Junior_
    c. the _Knorr_
    d. the _Nautile_

Answers

1. d; 2. d; 3. a; 4. b; 5. a; 6. b; 7. a; 8. a; 9. b; 10. a

Score Yourself

- If you got 8 or more correct, you are a **_Titanic_ Fanatic.**

- If you got 4 to 7 correct, you are a **Second Mate.**

- If you got 3 or fewer correct, you are just **Testing the Waters.**

the propellers and rudder of the _Titanic_ in dry dock

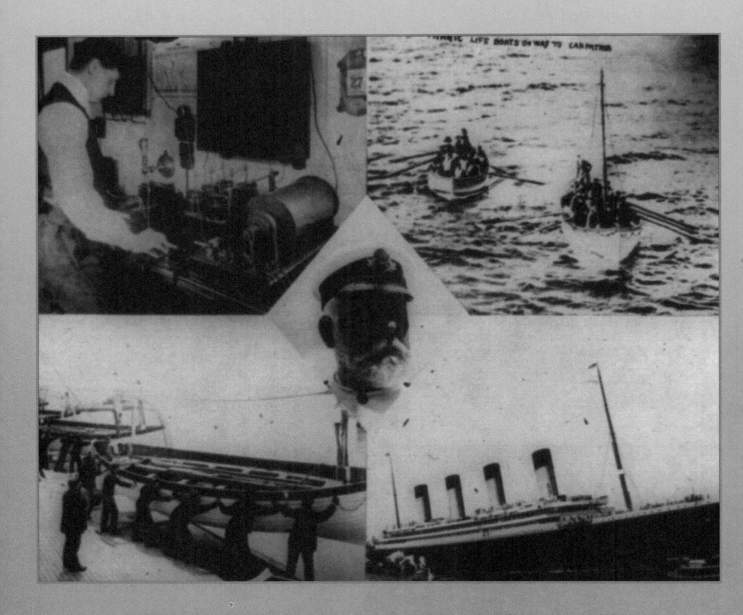

The Great Titanic Disaster

Wireless Operator on Shipboard receiving Distress Call

Life boats bringing Titanic's Survivors to the Carpathia

Capt. Smith of the Titanic

Life boat Drill   **The lost Liner**